What Happens

When You

DO

ANYTHING!

GW00372989

What Happens When You DO ANYTHING!

How to love life . . . and *enjoy* the Consequences!

ANDREW SERCOMBE

eagle

Guildford, Surrey

British Library Cataloguing in Publication Data. A catalogue record for this book is available from the British Library.

Published by Eagle Publishing Ltd, PO Box 530, Guildford, Surrey GU2 4FH.

Illustrations © 2001 Tim Charnick
Typeset by Eagle Publishing
Printed by Cox & Wyman, Reading
ISBN No: 0 86347 430 6

A Note from Me

Someone you know will love this book.

**It's about seeing life as it really is.
And accepting it.
And how to make it better.**

Whether you are tough or tender, old or young, a top executive or struggling at school, you can spread the word:

- It is more useful to be wise than merely clever
- Ignorance never was bliss
- The world is changed by ordinary people

Have *you noticed* what happens when you do ANYTHING?

Come on – let's get on with it!

Andrew Sercombe
andrew@powerchange.com

You change the future

Now you're not stuck with 'Fate', or lumbered with the potential liability of your birth date or star sign.

You no longer need to feel controlled by fortune telling, destiny or your horoscope.

You can go beyond that. You can learn new ways to actively influence the future, with *you* taking the initiative – and understanding what happens when you do. From now on you influence the future, not the other way round.

What might that be like?

Of course you won't want to BLAME 'fate' or 'the universe' or 'God' for what's happening to you, either. But that might just be progress.

This book is all about changing the future.
Your future.

It is about developing your thinking. It's about seeing things in a new, releasing, light. It's about living free and seeing possibilities.

Other people?
And it is about

ConSequences

I've used an upper case 'S' in the middle just to remind us:

something somewhere results from everything you do.

other people too – how their behaviour may affect you – and what you can do to either stop it affecting you negatively or make it work even better for you.

You don't have to live the way you are

now. You have a choice. Perhaps it's the ability to choose that makes us human beings human – and it is one of the most wonderful things in the world.

ConSequences

'Consequences' comes from two Latin words: *con* – with, *sequi* – to follow. In other words, what happens when you do ANYTHING!

- Work
- Home
- Social life
- Personal life

What you do today will be affected by what you've done before.

Everything you do tomorrow will be affected by what you did today.

Everything you do in the next ten years will be affected by what you've done in the last ten.

Just think what you can do to use that! When you discover the connections, you can change the world. Literally.

Your whole life is affected by what other people have done. Wouldn't it be great to know that you can change how you are affected by their actions?

So as you sit reading this book, you have been affected by the past and you will affect the future. In fact, simply reading this paragraph has changed you. What you think in the next few seconds will affect your life. It may be by a tiny amount or by more than you ever expected.

When a person realises how 'joined up' the world really is, what they do starts to take on a stronger meaning.

What about you?

Now?

Confidence – Reward – Guilt

The thought of others being affected by your actions can be very rewarding. If you are confident with the way you are living, you'll be happy both about being observed by the world around you and about affecting it.

If you are not confident that the way you are living is helpful to others, or has integrity, you are likely to experience a certain nagging guilt.

As you look around you every day, you can <u>see</u> the people whose lives are affected by the way you behave, the attitudes you take and the things you say.

'Do they trust me?'
People are more affected by what you *do*

than what you *say*. Where there is a credibility gap between what you do and what you say (what you do is different to what you say) they will trust you less. It might be worth asking, 'Is that what I want?' If the people who are watching you are children or your employees, they are likely to copy your behaviour to some extent. Their words and actions will lack credibility and trust largely because yours do.

'So what does all this mean?' you may ask. 'Do I now live in total fear just in case I do something that will hurt another person? Or would it be better to bury my head in the sand and live with a couldn't care less attitude?'

Up a tree

Those are two extreme positions and extremes aren't usually too helpful. For instance, our children, when they were quite small used to love climbing the trees in our garden. Occasionally they would fall and sometimes hurt themselves.

However, to stop them climbing those trees would have been very limiting for them and would have cramped their wonderful spirit of adventure. We didn't want to do that, so we encouraged them to climb carefully and taught them how. We made them aware of possible dangers.

Result?

> **The answer to misuse is rarely non-use; it's CORRECT USE**

- They didn't fall and hurt themselves so often.
- They learnt that the answer to misuse is rarely non use; it's CORRECT USE.

14

How your life affects other people

Whether or not you are proud of the way you live, you are responsible for how your life affects other people. You are responsible for what people pick up from you. They have a responsibility towards you too. Becoming aware of consequences means that we live a little bit more awake to the effect of our life. And when you become skilled at seeing what happens when you behave in a particular way, it is amazing how much good you can do to benefit others and make the world a better place.

What to do when you do not like the way you live:

Change it.

'Just a minute!' I can hear you say. 'Nothing in life is as easy as that. I've tried to change, and I can't.'

- Perhaps you tried to change too much at a time.
- Perhaps you didn't see how much it would be to your advantage to change.
- Perhaps you tried to change something that, in your heart of hearts, you wanted to keep.

It is perfectly possible for you to make small changes that will make a huge difference to your life. In my Powerchange Coaching practice I use the phrase, 'Gain without Pain'. Those changes do not need to be painful, in fact they can be very rewarding indeed.

- Imagine making changes to your life that have a huge beneficial impact.
- Imagine what it might be like to know that the changes you have made were really good ones.
- Imagine how satisfying it might be to see

other people changing for the better just because you did!

So what would you like to change? What might a first step towards making that change be? Just a very small step. Perhaps even a smaller step than the one you just thought of. Choose a step that you *know* is possible for you and you really want! (There is no point in trying to take steps that you neither want nor believe you can achieve.)

In Your Control

Up to 90 per cent of what you do and think today is virtually the same as what you did and thought yesterday, and it produces the same results. If you really like all those results, great! If you would like to control those results, read on.

- We have already seen that *you can* change your world and *you do so* every day.
- You make it better or worse. You make it more interesting, or
- more boring. It is as it is right now because of you.

You can change the world you live in by making different decisions to the ones you made yesterday and acting on them.

- The decisions that will change your life the most are those you make **deliberately** and usually **'out of character'**.
- It is only such decisions that will make your life different from the way it has been.
- Most significant changes are initiated by developments outside your sphere of control.

'Matt's Exciting Day'

Matt got out of bed every morning a few minutes after the alarm sang its merry tune.

He never got out straightaway because he liked a few minutes to bask in the luxury of a warm bed before facing the day.

He went to the bathroom, showered with the water at the usual temperature, shaved with his familiar shaving gel and dressed in his normal work clothes.

He drove his car to work on his standard route and arrived at the office at the usual time.

Hanging his coat on the peg he

always used, he sat at his own desk and faced the same computer screen. He booted it up. It was in its ordinary position with its familiar screen saver. It was 8.30 am and he was already bored.

Matt's strategy

Matt tried to keep things in their normal routine so that the day would be free from too many hassles. That way he would be able to get through the day and earn enough money to keep the pension fund up and accrue some savings to take his family to the same resort in the Mediterranean that they always go to.

Of course, life for Matt could be different. Instead of getting through his work so that he can enjoy himself doing what he wants at the weekend, or in that two weeks in the Med. or when he retires, he could

Matt re-checked his strategy, "28 years x
52 weeks x 5 days x 8 hours less two
weeks each year in Torremolinos"

enjoy his work every day.

Every day!

Let's take a closer look at Matt's habits.

What would happen if . . .

- He set the alarm an hour earlier and read?

- Or did some physical exercise before he went to work?

- Or drove a different route?

- Or decided to see how many amusing signs he could find on the way to work – just for a laugh?

What would happen if . . .

- He arranged to meet a friend at the office for a coffee before work?

- Or swapped chairs with another person in the office for a morning (with their consent of course!)

What would happen if . . .

He decided he could write a book on . . . anything . . . whether or not it got published?

A personal example
Only a year or so ago I had never seriously thought anything I wrote would ever be published, but as I write, this is the FOURTH book that I have been asked for! One of my publishers said last week that they expect me to write one every six

months. Needless to say, my life is not boring – and both Matt and you can have a different life too if you want.

Habits that work

For the most part, people assume that change must be a bad thing and don't want it. They have very good reasons – at least, they are very good reasons from their own point of view! Matt kept to his own carefully planned and controlled routine because *he believed it to be the least painful way of getting through life*. And it worked, to a degree. It did get him through and it wasn't too painful.

Ritual brain numbing

In fact, the ritual of getting to work could be done with his brain in 'automatic', and the result was very satisfactorily numbing from where he saw it. However, to live like that for the most of the year in order to be able to go on holiday for just a couple of weeks seems an extraordinary waste of a good life to me.

ConSequences . . .

> **Boring job > brain numbing strategy > two weeks of pleasure > out of money, so back to > same boring job**

Is that what you want your entire life to consist of? What else might there be instead?

Jonathan

Jonathan is in his twenties. His strategy for life is quite different. He has chosen, as a basic and essential policy for his life, to be as fully 'in touch' with life as he can.

One attitude that is important to him is to be always learning (one of his one-liners is 'I am a learning organisation!') and to benefit from everything that life throws at him. A favourite quote is 'If you can't kill me you can only improve me'. And he means it.

Jonathan is never bored for long because he will immediately engage with the source of his boredom and turn it around, see it differently, be creative with it. A repetitive task will be turned into a mental competition with himself. Can he do this faster or improve the process? Or he will use his brain for something else while he is doing the boring task.

For you and me this may seem a tiring way to live. For Jonathan it is an essential way to live. He loves living 'on the edge'. I know him well – his life is definitely not boring! This is how one woman changes things around:

*Half the week I commute a long dis-
tance to work by train and love the
chance this gives me to read all sorts
of books. I escape to almost anywhere, a battlefield, foreign parts,
even the inside of a murderer's mind.*

Today I was in a hospital waiting to see a
consultant. So many of those waiting had
bored and irritated looks on their faces.
They could have been using their lives in a
thousand different ways, but just hadn't
thought how. Because of the delay in the
waiting area I have another thousand words
typed out on my discreet little handheld
computer and you are reading them right
now.

ConSequences . . .

**Potentially boring wait > an idea
buzzing that needs to be captured >**

**a few pounds worth of technology >
a chunk of a book written > no
boring wait.**

Living with consequences

As we have seen, every decision we make,
or choose not to make, has consequences.
An important part of being mature is to be
able to look ahead and forecast what may
happen if we make a particular decision. It
is to do with time.

You may well have heard this intriguing
story ...

*Richard Cannon-Smythe was a self-
made multi-millionaire businessman.
He admired himself every morning
and gave the impression, not least
to himself, that everything was possible if you were smart enough. His
latest project was property and he*

had recently discovered that Seamus O'Reilly, the old Irishman in the next village had a delightful little site for a new housing estate. The only problem would be to convince Seamus to sell.

Seamus utterly refused. 'I'm terribly sorry to disappoint you, Richard, me old friend,' he said in his Limerick accent. 'But this land has belonged to me father and his father before him. I couldn't sell to you.' Furious, the property developer upped his offer from the pittance he had first suggested. No luck.

Over the next few months he upped his offer very close to his limit. Eventually Seamus O'Reilly yielded, on one condition: he would be paid the money up-front and in full, but could have just one more crop off the field. Richard Cannon-Smythe was delighted. He thought of the money he would make on this field in just a year or so and congratulated himself on being so smart once more. The documents were drawn up, and after careful examination, Seamus signed them. The deal was done. He had just one crop to plant and harvest and the field would be gone. He went to bed that night smiling quietly to himself.

The next day, Richard was in good spirits and popped along to the local paper. He wanted full coverage for this outstanding venture – he loved publicity. He picked up the editor (who didn't particularly like Richard Cannon-Smythe, but did fancy a free gourmet lunch) and decided to drive him past the green-field site in his Rolls-Royce on their way to the restaurant. The figure of the little old Irishman could be seen at work in the hazy winter sun. The two men got out of the Rolls and wandered over to the little old man.

It was at this precise moment that Richard Cannon-Smythe's life passed before his eyes. He let out an uncontrollable cry of anguish.

Seamus O'Reilly was planting . . . acorns.

ConSequences . . .

Of course you don't need me to tell you that a forest of oak trees takes about 200 years to grow.

* Richard Cannon-Smythe never did get his field.

- Nor would his children after him.
- Seamus O'Reilly's children would, on the other hand, be remarkably well provided for!
- The local paper had a perfect story that sold them thousands more copies, and got them onto national television evening news.
- Richard Cannon-Smythe, the millionaire property developer, was the laughing-stock of the county, was not seen in public for months and eventually went bankrupt.

Apart from the obvious lesson 'Never underestimate the business skill of an Irishman', there is a lot we can gather from this fable. Here are three of them:

1. Things often do not work out quite as we expect.
2. The next generation may well be affected by our decisions.

'Outcome' his grandfather had said,
'Outcome is everything.'

3. Time is an essential ingredient in
   Consequences Thinking.

Time

Time matters to us. Our lives consist of it. We devised time so that we could measure ourselves and our universe.

We describe where we are in life using a scale of time. And trying to 'turn the clock back' is merely a sentimental emptiness which in itself wastes time.

Outside time

Religions of the world highlight the importance of an understanding of time and attempt to put it into some sort of context. I am committed to my Christian faith, and know that a concept of 'eternity' – not so much endless time, but an environment outside time – is essential to the framework in which Christianity functions.

Of course some who read this will think

that how we spend our lives is not important, that 'wasting time' doesn't matter. Time is ours to waste. 'It is up to me to do what I like with my life.' Yet deep inside we are uncomfortably aware that it does matter really. Most of us want our lives to be productive and useful, even though some may give up on this quest and choose to live purely for their own pleasure.

Protection racket

You may know people who spend their lives staving off anything they do not want to face – however true or real it is. Do you know anyone like that? The pursuit of personal pleasure can be used as a huge cover-up. Like the committed drug addict, you can damn your future for a few more hours blotting out the pain.

We all know how a 'protection racket' works:

People pay out huge sums of money to people they don't like to keep those same people from hurting them. Are you paying out your life to something you don't particularly care for in order to make yourself feel better for a while?

Food

Food can be like that. The consequences of eating to make youself feel better or to take your mind off an unhappy situation are just the opposite of what you want: more unhappiness.

Retail Therapy

In my Powerchange Life Coaching clinics I see people who are in serious debt. 'Comfort shopping' – an attempt to cheer them up for a bit (and it does on the surface) – ends up with more debt, and higher

payments, and more credit cards, and . . .
you know the story.

Image
How do you see yourself – or think other
people see you? As you get older, how are
you going to handle the changes? Facelift?
Nips and tucks? Acting 'young'? Of course
no one wants to appear thirty when they're
only sixteen. Or sixty years old when
they're forty-five. But do we want to spend
our lives with the stress of trying to be
something we're not? Some people are so
afraid of death they kill themselves trying
to avoid it.

Enjoy who you are now. Take full advantage of the time you have today. Use it well
and live without regrets. You'll not need any
dubious protection that way.

ConSequences . . .

You feel you are misusing your life > as a result you feel empty and sad > so you blot out the reality using your favourite method > and more of your energy and time is wasted > so you feel even more sad and empty > you have to blot out even more reality > etc.

What might an alternative look like?

You have a clear sense of personal purpose > and you start to act on that sense of purpose > which makes you feel increasingly good and 'rewarded' by your actions > so you act some more towards your purpose > etc.

Revealing the value

In these two options, time plays the all-important part of revealing the value of our actions. You will already be able to look back over your life and see consequences of your actions, even consequences of your thinking. Serious thinking inevitably results in a change of projected behaviour, however subtle.

Brainpower

You become what you think, and what you think affects everything else.

'How does my thinking and behaviour affect other people?'

This all seems very obvious. Yet what is obvious after you think about it isn't quite so obvious before you do! Have you ever thought about the way you have behaved over the years? What was the outcome of your actions?

ConSequences . . .

Here is another little ConSequence based on fact:

> **Boy loves football > plays and practices a lot > gets selected for school side > eventually becomes national player > earns lots of money > eventually retires from national game at thirty-two years old > develops pain in knees four years later > crippled for life > lives in a wheelchair > entire family affected > wishes he had never played football — ever.**

Perhaps you could do with a more encouraging sequence!

Here is a true story which shows that even something that seems tragic can be turned into something useful.

Joni Eareckson loved swimming > at the age of nineteen she dived into water that was too shallow and broke her neck > became a quadriplegic for life > she asked herself 'Why am I alive?' > found the answer > now lives in a wheelchair > started to live for others (including writing her book *Joni*) > has seen thousands of other people choose to live less selfish lives because of her story.

Or this one that was in the newspaper today:

Sixty young professionals leave their beautiful homes and move into an area of Manchester, England, that is so run down that estate agents frequently offer clients a second house thrown in at half price > they commit themselves to living there for life – as missionaries > the entire housing estate starts to change with broken glass, gangs and boarded up houses being replaced by trimmed hedges and litter-free streets > crime levels fall including drugs and prostitution > house prices rise > the desperation of the estate changes to dignity and self-respect.

(*Weekend Telegraph*, 8.7.00)

What are the consequences that other people have to handle because you have behaved in a particular way?

Do you take them into consideration at all?

On a scale of 1–10, how much?

Changing *your* mind changes the world

Chris is a quiet thoughtful man, not given to too much display of emotion. He and Denise have two children, six and nine years old. He is a consultant with a big firm in the City. Last week he came home from work to his normally bubbly wife who greeted him with 'I can't live with you any more. I want us to split up and you to leave the home as soon as possible.'

Chris was dumbfounded and bewildered. Where on earth did that come from? Without going into the details of this particular incident, or attributing blame, we can certainly assume a number of ConSequential things:

This is no unthought-out decision on the woman's part. Spontaneous though she may be, she has thought long and hard about this one.

The signs have probably been around for five years if the husband had been tuned to them.

There is no 'single issue' decision.

She has taken an 'I-have-no-choice' stance, which may not be the best way to solve her perceived problems.

They both feel desperate and trapped.

They will both experience significant emotional and 'spiritual' pain.

The children will suffer.

Their wider family and friends will hurt too.

The eventual Bang!

As we have already established earlier in this book, when we act in a particular way nothing may happen to start with.

When I was a teenager I went to a brilliant school lecture given by an explosives expert. It was great fun to see the scientist mixing chemicals together in particular quantities and then carrying on with his talk. Nothing seemed to be happening, until for no obvious reason, there was a mighty bang! As he was talking the liquids were mixing together until they reached a critical point and ... BANG!

He knew it would explode.

We did too.

We just didn't know quite when!

Eventually you will see **the results of your actions. ACT towards your goal and there will be a result.**

However, we are not always that good at looking. Timing matters too. Results do not always occur when we expect. They often happen much later. It is well known that even top researchers tend to see just the things that they are looking for and miss seeing other things that are happening. Be careful to look.

'It's not what your vision is, it's what it does . . .'

Vision is one of those overworked words bandied about by 'forward thinkers'. It has the strange effect of being both exciting and irritating.

Vision is the ability to see.

'I can see this is going to be really good for you.'

'From my point of view this is going to be a disaster.'

'Thanks for explaining – I can see that now.'

'I can just see him doing that!'
Most of us have the ability to picture in our mind's eye what something may be like. The amazing thing about imagination is how we can use it, and when we use it to 'see' something about ourselves in the present, or a possibility in the future, change isn't far away. 'Seeing' has consequences. Not 'seeing' does too.

Doing the right things guarantees success

When you do the right things you will succeed!

- Sometimes you will need to **be persistent.**
- Sometimes you will need to **wait.**
- Sometimes you may need **some help** – but success is heading in your direction.

It is easy to be so focused on doing things dead right that we don't realise what we are doing is dead wrong! There is no long-term vantage in being perfect at deceiving people, at shop lifting, or at something 'innocent' like eating an unbalanced diet. There will be consequences, and I won't like them!

Doing the wrong thing very successfully

The Hudson Bay Company once recorded men starving to death even though they caught and ate rabbits. They became very clever at catching rabbits to provide essential food – but despite eating lots of rabbit meat, many men died. Why? Because we human beings use more vitamins to digest rabbits than we gain from eating them. These men literally ate themselves to death. They did the wrong thing, catching and eating rabbits, very well.

And then there was the expert manager

He prided himself at being utterly brilliant at what he did, and like the Hudson Bay rabbit catchers, ended up with a lot of regrets – for about fifteen years.

His special skill was faking banknotes.

It is quite possible to do all these things to perfection, yet do a lot of harm, or simply not get the consequences we want. You may get what you want, but there again, you may win the lottery – provided you fill in the ticket to perfection. . .

Wait for it . . .

When nothing seems to happen it may be that what you did hasn't worked; or it may just be that it hasn't worked YET. There is all the difference in the world.

Officer McDonald realised his hunch was right.
It had no watermark.

When consequences don't show up . . . yet

She wrote this brief and succinct letter to the Problem Page:

'I am sixteen. Can you help me?'

The Agony Aunt replied, 'Wait a while and it will go away.'

It did.

You and I live in what is called 'a closed system'. You can't get off the train! Someone, somewhere, will always live with the consequences of what you do with what you have, and it may be you.

Margaret has quietly stashed away a few pounds every month in a well-managed fund since she first started work years ago. Back then it was quite a sacrifice out of her pay packet each week. Now she doesn't even notice it. When she retires she will never have to think about money again. She'll be very happy to live with the consequences!

Jack has kept a close eye on his physical health over six decades. Apart from one or two injuries he is fitter than I am – and thirty years older.

Amy has worked on the Consequences principle too. She chose her degree with an eye to the future and worked very hard through university, graduating well. Her company keep asking her what she would like to do for them next! Others in the industry are constantly after her commitment, knowledge and skills.

On the other hand, not everything goes quite so well . . .

We live in a society that is now very conscious of ecological consequences. We worry about the future of our plants, animals and our environment in general. Thirty years ago it was different. No one cared. We are picking up the bill for our attitudes then. Literally 'picking up the bill' – it is costing us all billions to clean up the mess.

The Twelve Steps of the Shower Progression

Have you ever heard of the Shower Progression? You've probably experienced it without knowing!

1. There you are in an unfamiliar shower, and the water is a bit cool, so . . .
2. You turn up the dial. Nothing happens.
3. You turn it up some more. Nothing happens.

4. You turn it up some more.
5. All of a sudden the water gets hotter from the first change.
6. And hotter still from the second change.
7. *We're not through yet – there's still even hotter water to come!* In a desperate bid to protect yourself . . .
8. You panic, grab the dial and turn it down – a lot. But nothing happens.
9. So you turn it down a lot more.
10. Then freezing water gushes over your hot body.
11. Now in a different sort of agony, you grab the dial and turn it back up . . .
12. Or just quit!

The reason for this jarring experience is that there is a **time delay** on the results of turning the dial. You'll get what you want, but not just yet. Your brain does not immediately account for this and assumes,

Connie's daily shower was well known
in Meadow Crescent

wrongly, that nothing is happening. Something *is* happening, of course, but you don't know about it yet – until it is too late!

The same thing happens when steering a large ship. Turn the helm (or whatever it's called these days) and nothing happens, or so it seems. But something is happening, it just isn't obvious yet. Before long there is an almost imperceptible change

What mountains do you have?

Is it to do with your family?

A relationship?

A habit you want moved?

A qualification?

A financial mountain?

Make the decision

Start

of direction, then some more, until the ship is clearly on a different course.

A few months ago I was worried about an aspect of my business. Although I knew I was 'doing the right things' nothing seemed to be happening. I discussed this with my son, Jonathan. 'Dad,' he said, 'you choose long-term strategies and look for short-term results!' And he was right. If you want short-term results you employ short-term strategies. Using the ship illustration again, if you want to turn around very quickly on the water, don't become a captain of a super-tanker, go for a jet-ski.

Big things have momentum and it takes time for them to change direction.

- The effects of the way *your parents* lived will show up in *their grandchildren* – thirty years later.

- Violence on the streets starts with
  violence in the home – ten, twenty,
  thirty years ago.

Work at it

Q.	**How do you move a mountain?**
A.	**A bucketful at a time.**

There is a lot of difference between looking at what you've done and saying 'nothing's changed. I'll do something else'; and
saying, 'There has been a tiny change, do I
want more of it?'

The smallest change ever can be *doubled* by
doing what caused that small change one
more time – 100 per cent increase! The
casual observer may not see the changes.
The unconcerned bystander may not notice

any difference. But carefully trained senses can pick up changes that may go unnoticed by others.

Moving Mountains

I come across all sorts of people who have decided that a particular mountain must move – and they have the faith to believe it will eventually. With little fuss and no big pronouncements they get their bucket and spade and start moving it. That mountain may be huge – a cure for cancer, or something like that – but they start.

A year later, nothing seems to have changed.

Five years later a small indent in the mountain has appeared.

Ten years later and there seems to be a substantial team, other men and women

who have seen that the mountain needs to
be moved.

Twenty years, perhaps thirty, and the
mountain hasn't gone yet but it certainly
looks different.

The original person with the idea of moving the mountain dies, but the mountain
continues to be moved by those who
caught the vision.

Slavery, apartheid, polio and a thousand other
evil mountains have been moved this way.

Faith-filled people move mountains.

A bucketful at a time.

Evidence
It takes special people to affect the world
this way.

People like you.
What will happen when YOU decide to make decisions that have consequences like those?

If you were going to devote yourself to changing something that was bigger than you but needed to be changed, what would it be?

When would you start?

What plan would you begin with? Some changes yield best to proper planning – in fact most things do. Unfortunately it is extraordinarily easy to get so focused on what you are planning to do that it never actually gets done.

One reason for this is that as we look at the size of the change we get completely intimidated by it, defeated by the enormity of the task.

'The mountain will need a lot more than my bucket and spade, more than my energies.'

'How silly I will look as I make such a small impression on such a colossal undertaking.'

Remember my comments earlier on in this book about what you think will affect the future? 'Can't' thinking has stopped millions of things being done. 'I can't do it,' we think. And we don't. Have you said that in the last week?

This is what happens inside your brain when you say 'I can't'

'Can't' is a very interesting word. It is an abbreviation in English for cannot, or can not.

Let's look at your defeating sentence again.

'I can't do it.'

'I cannot do it.'

'I can not do it.'

'I CAN not do it.'

And because we *can* NOT do it, that is exactly what we do: not do it. When that is your decision you suddenly are rewarded with an odd sort of success. You have actually managed NOT to do it very successfully indeed — in fact you haven't even started to do it!

'It took me five hours!' Corinne was laughing as she told me.

But this 46-year-old *did actually run* the 26 km course. The sense of achievement was written all over her face. She'd never run that distance before, and had been training for 6 months.

What a success! What a woman.

What power!

How very successful!

The deed has, in fact, been completely *not* done.

And it was YOU that managed to *not* do it! Brilliant.

Sort of.

100% success . . . sort of

The consequence of your decision is: nothing was done – with 100 per cent success.

Nothing happened. Big time.

What is it that you have managed successfully to not do?

I have watched teenagers, mostly competitive young men, but girls too, decide that *they cannot afford to be seen to fail* or do something imperfectly because they will be teased, or laughed at, or may not 'shine'. Better to be told off for not doing it. That way no one will know you couldn't.

Hundreds of thousands of exams have been missed on that basis . . .

Here's how:
The reasoning goes like this: 'I can handle getting into trouble for missing the exam, but I cannot possibly handle being seen to **fail** it. Failing it has no pleasure for me at all. If I fail, it shows I'm a failure, I'm not intelligent, I'm lazy or I have wasted my time. If I **miss** the exam I can think up a good excuse that puts me in a much better light. I was ill. The transport broke down/didn't come. At least it won't be my fault then.'

BLAME AND GRATITUDE

It is easy to find someone to blame. And if they're really stuck, quite a few people are quick to blame God.

I've got an interest in that perspective because, as you know, mine is a predominantly Christian view of the world. God is the spiritual focus of my life. I'm interested in the way that although God seems to gets the blame he gets very little credit. When a friend dies of an unexplained disease: that's God's fault. When I live a full, healthy life: well, that's not God, that's because I look after myself. (Or perhaps it was just Lucky, whoever Lucky is.)

If we are choosing to blame others for things that go wrong, whether that is God or the Government or anyone else, it seems only fair to be even-handed and give them the credit for all the myriad of things we don't notice go well every day. And be grateful to them.

Much less painful.

Short term.

Long term? Well, what are the consequences of not having the qualification?

I can make some guesses.

I suspect you can too.

Attributed to . . .

Have you noticed how consequences seem
so much more bearable if it's not your
fault? It is a huge relief when it is actually
somebody else's fault.

- Your future promotion will not be
   affected.
- It's not your name that will appear in
   the press.

- You won't be disciplined.

Negative attribution

What are the consequences of making sure someone else is blamed for something you have done, or neglected to do?

The truth is, blaming doesn't work — unless the intention is for you to feel better and other people to pay for your mistakes.

The Scapegoat

The up side of blaming other people is that the same outward results are seen and you go free:

- Your future promotion will *not* be affected.
- It's *not* your name that will appear in the press.
- You *won't* be disciplined.

But there's more isn't there.

The downside is that for the rest of your life someone else will be on your conscience. Your refusal to accept responsibility means that others are forced to take responsibility that does not belong to them.

Is there a situation in your life where you are blaming others for something deep down you know you were responsible for?

What would it take to put it right?

What would the long-term consequences be of correcting the impression that they were to blame, when they weren't?

There is nothing quite so releasing as the truth. When you choose to live in a truthful way, your life becomes a whole lot less complicated and other people live freer too.

Positive attribution

I will never forget the powerful feelings of pride as I watched my children receive their university degrees. The ceremony was preceded by three years, probably six or eight actually, of hard work as they achieved the necessary school grades and then the sweat of studying at university. The culmination of all this determined application is an excited phone call on the morning the results are pinned up on the appropriate notice-board in the faculty hall. Next comes the Graduation Ceremony a few weeks later, with all its colourful gowns, hoods, mortarboards and music. Proud parents gather with their son or daughter for the day and make their way to the Great Hall for the presentations. There follows about two hours of applause, honouring all those young men and women (mostly young, anyway!) whose hard work is eventually being recognised. I absolutely loved each of those days. I was a really proud Dad!

Praise

It would be hard to over-estimate the positive effect of praise. All of us know just how good it is to be honoured in front of others for our achievements. From the earliest moments of our lives praise has played a most significant part. In the short-term culture around us in Britain in these first years of the new millennium praise has been replaced by demand for more.

Praise *pleasure*

In a recent class I was teaching, one of the members of the group was constantly critical of others, picking fault on whatever was done – however well. I talked privately to this person about the sheer pleasure of giving unqualified praise. I helped him identify the feeling of pleasure he could experience. I suggested to him that he went round the room to the other people in the class and looked for things he could praise them for, and then praised them sincerely in an appropriate way. To his credit he listened to what I said and tried the experiment. I heard him giving each person one or two encouraging comments. It made a difference to him – and to the class. (A week later he was praising me – and asking if I had noticed!) Good on him.

Try it

You can try the experiment too. The longer you do it the greater the pleasure you'll experience. Try it for an hour, a whole day, a week or the rest of your life.

How much 'praise pleasure' will you allow yourself to enjoy and to give? Is praise something that you believe is in limited supply and must therefore be rationed? Perhaps it would be a lot more useful to attribute a belief like that to something that's damaging.

What do you imagine the consequences of your praising will be for the people you are praising?

In the trade that might just be termed win/win!

Joe – a true story

I was reading this challenging life story
again recently.

> Joe grew up in a big, unconvention-
> al family (to say the least!). His
> father had several children from
> each of four women. He was mar-
> ried to two of them.

> Joe's dad, Jake, was a shrewd
> dealer, having learned as a teenag-
> er from Joe's grandmother how to
> rip people off. Twenty years later
> Joe was born to his dad's favourite
> woman.

> By this time Jake was very rich. He
> and his family spent quite a lot of
> time avoiding the people he had
> ripped off, some of whom made it

very clear they wanted him . . .
somewhere else. Joe's own uncle,
for instance (one of the first people
his dad ever exploited), had issued
a death threat years before Joe was
born. It had never been withdrawn.

Joe's brothers were messed up and
vicious people. When Joe's only sis-
ter was raped, they massacred not
just the man himself but all the men
in his widespread family 'for treating
our sister like a prostitute'.

When Joe was still quite small, Jake
decided to attempt a return to the
substantial family ranch, his boy-
hood home, where his estranged
and angry brother was farming.

Deep inside he wanted peace, and
here the story takes a twist for the
better (it could do with it!)

*One dark night, when he was proba-
bly at the lowest point in his life, Jake
had a powerful encounter with a person he met on the banks of the nearby river. They started to struggle, and
as they did so, Jake became more
and more convinced in his mind that
this person was supernatural, perhaps even God . He fought most of
the night, with Jake being physically
as well as emotionally affected.
Something 'snapped' inside, and he
knew he would never be the same
person again. Although he physically
limped for the rest of his life, Jake
was a different man. Out of the blue,
Jake's brother, Joe'' uncle, sponta-
neously forgave him, Jake bought a
large family ranch fairly nearby, and
they settled down.*

*Although they were a pretty nasty
family by most standards (they were*

driven by fear, and displays of jealousy and violent anger were rife – you wouldn't want them living anywhere near you!), as Joe grew up, his reaction to his home life was interesting. He reacted AWAY FROM the conniving and scheming business methods of his father and the violent lifestyle of his brothers TOWARDS a surprising openness and honesty in his relationships. This was completely out of character from most of his family.

In his teens Joe himself was abducted and sold by migrant traders to an autocratic high-up government minister in a foreign nation. Despite a spell in prison (for NOT sleeping with the boss's wife) Joe finally ended up in the highest echelons of government and eventually ran the country, honoured and admired by all.

What a way to live!

Don't waste your life making excuses for your behaviour, perhaps citing your upbringing, education or background. It is **how you choose to react** to that background, not the background itself, that will largely decide your destiny.

- You can influence the consequences of the future by living wisely now.
- You can use your upbringing as an excuse for the way you live: 'I can't help it, I was brought up like this.'
- You can use your past as a resource for a better future: 'This is the way I'm going to be. I will not blame others for who I am.'